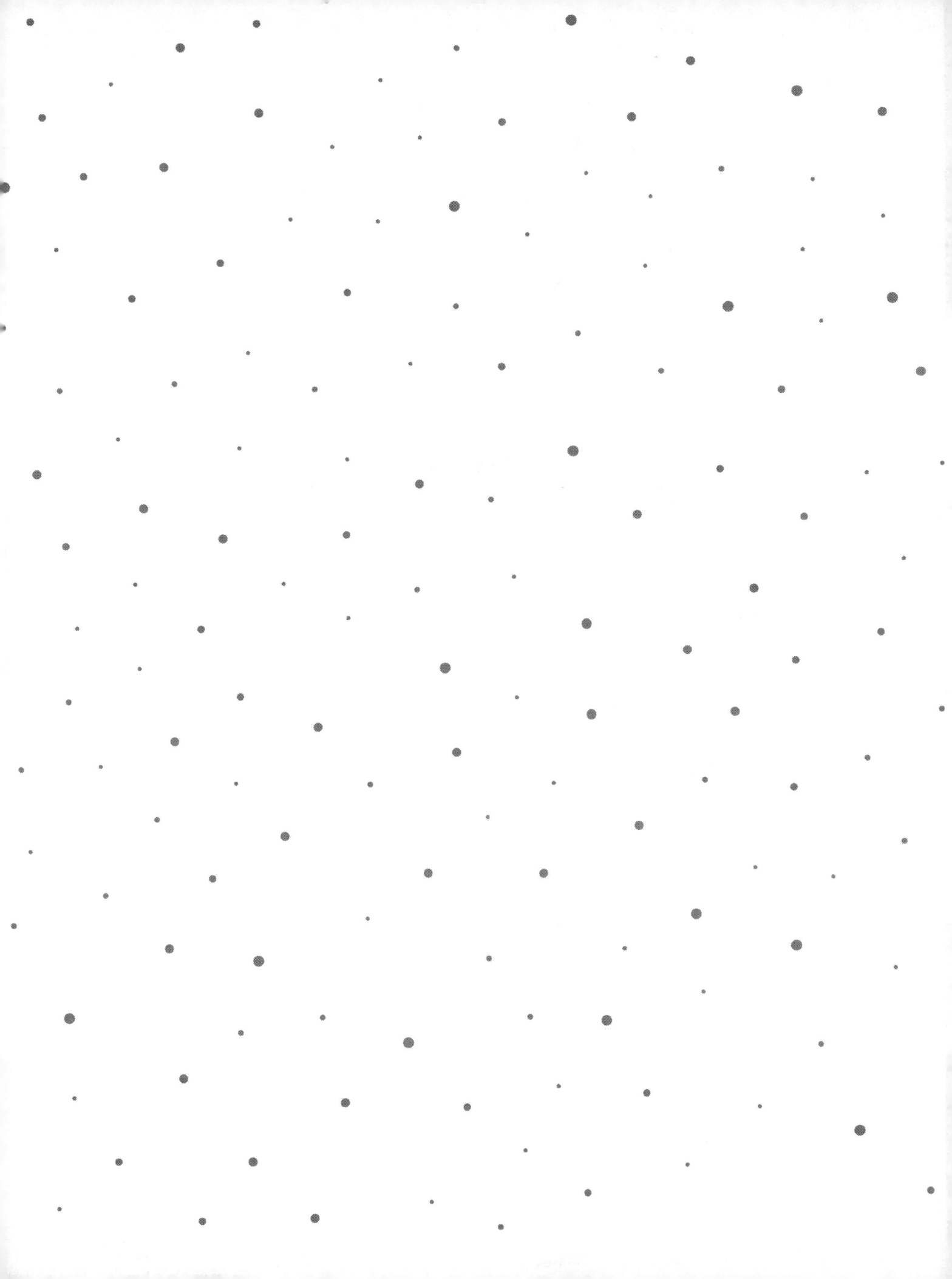

Modern Cursive for Teens

CURSIVE PRACTICE WITH OVER 200 WORDS. LETTERS, PHRASES. INSPIRATIONAL LYRICS. AND MOTIVATIONAL PROMPTS FOR FUN, RELAXING CURSIVE HANDWRITING TO IMPROVE YOUR PENMANSHIP

COLLECT ALL FOUR

MODERN CURSIVE HANDWRITING WORKBOOK FOR ADULTS

MODERN CURSIVE HANDWRITING WORKBOOK FOR TEENS

MODERN CALLIGRAPHY HANDWRITING WORKBOOK

MODERN CALLIGRAPHY LETTERING AND NUMBERS PRACTICE

This Penmanship Workbook

Belongs to:

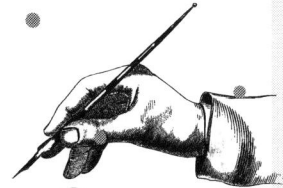

Table of Contents

Introduction   03

Part 1
Practice Lettering   07

Part 2
Practice 1-2 words   43

Part 3
Practice Writing Through Famous Quotes   53

Part 4
Practice with Famous Song Lyrics   59

Part 5
Motivational Quotes   71

Part 6
Practice with Modern Cursive Styles   85

Part 6
Extra Practice on Your Own   97

Tools Needed

Practicing Modern Cursive doesn't require a fountain pen or ink bottle.

Instead, we recommend any of the following pens, although basic felt tip pens work just fine, too:

- Calligraphy Pens
- Pencils
- Brush Markers
- Broad Edge Pens and Markers
- Felt Tip and Flat Pens

All of the above can be found at Amazon or at your local craft store.

Where has all the cursive gone?

Hi, my name is Brie. I am a psychologist, a mother, and a self-admitted non-cursive user. Over the years, my cursive writing has slowly dwindled away, resulting in my current blend (sometimes legible) print/cursive/scribble script.

As a parent, I see that my children are barely taught this in elementary school. It's not required later in life; teachers don't ask for it, so we have developed the lost art of basic cursive.

After researching, I verified that the best way to retrain our brains to incorporate this lost art is through repetition, repetition, and more repetition. Although I try to avoid the boredom of repeating a letter 1000 times, I created this book to include basic letters, tracing, letter building, and application through motivational and inspirational quotes.

I know we do not all prefer a one-size-fits-all formal cursive writing style, so I incorporated a selection of traditional and modern styles to work from.

Please take your time, relax on the couch, sit back, and try your hand at the lost art of beautiful cursive writing.

~ Brie @ Creative Works Books

Cursive Fun Facts

Cursive writing is a unique form of writing that is becoming less common as time goes by, as more people are adopting typing and printing as their preferred means of communication. However, there are still many reasons why cursive writing is valuable and essential to learn.

Fact #1: Research has shown that cursive writing can help develop fine motor skills. Forming the letters in cursive requires more hand and finger movements than printing, which can help children, teens, adults and seniors develop hand-eye coordination and dexterity.

Fact #2: Cursive writing can improve writing speed and efficiency. Since cursive letters are joined together, writing in cursive can be faster than printing. This is especially useful for students who need to take notes quickly or for professionals who need to write rapidly and efficiently.

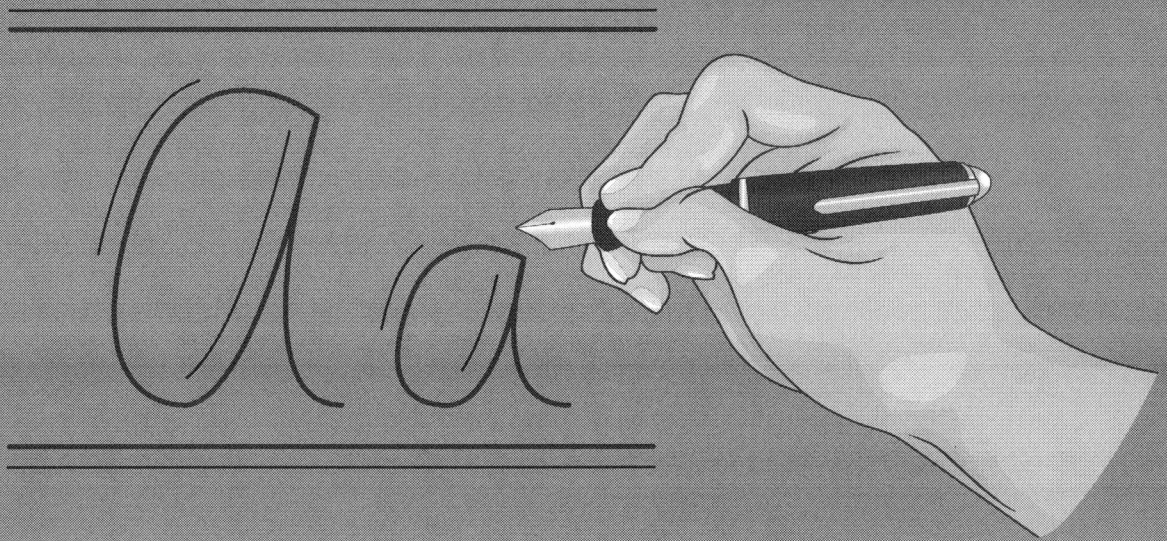

FACT #3: Cursive writing can add a personal touch to a letter or report. A handwritten letter in cursive can convey a sense of warmth, personality, and intimacy that cannot be replicated in a typed letter. In addition, many historical documents were written in cursive, and being able to read and write in cursive can help us better understand and appreciate these essential pieces of history.

Cursive writing may not be as necessary as it once was, but there are still many reasons why it is valuable and I essential to learn. It can help with fine motor skills, improve writing speed and efficiency, and add a personal touch to our writing.

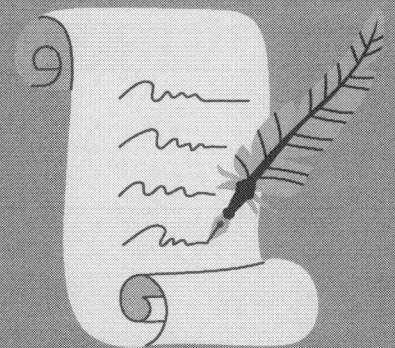

PART 1

Practice Lettering

Practice tracing and writing the various letters. Be mindful of your pen stroke and rhythm as you trace the letters. Practice as many times as you'd like.

a

B

B B B B B B

B B B B B B

B B B B B B B B B

B B B B B B B B B

B B B B B B B B B

b

b b b b b b

b b b b b b

b b b b b b b b b

b b b b b b b b b

b b b b b b b b b

9

C

e e e e e e e

e e e e e e e

e e e e e e e e

e e e e e e e e

e e e e e e e e

C

b b b b b b

b b b b b b

b b b b b b b b b

b b b b b b b b b

b b b b b b b b b

D

D D D D D D
D D D D D D

D D D D D D D D D D
D D D D D D D D D D
D D D D D D D D D D

d

d d d d d d
d d d d d d

d d d d d d d d d d
d d d d d d d d d d
d d d d d d d d d d

$\mathcal{E}$

$\mathcal{E}$ $\mathcal{E}$ $\mathcal{E}$ $\mathcal{E}$ $\mathcal{E}$ $\mathcal{E}$

$\mathcal{E}$ $\mathcal{E}$ $\mathcal{E}$ $\mathcal{E}$ $\mathcal{E}$ $\mathcal{E}$

$\mathcal{E}$ $\mathcal{E}$ $\mathcal{E}$ $\mathcal{E}$ $\mathcal{E}$ $\mathcal{E}$ $\mathcal{E}$ $\mathcal{E}$ $\mathcal{E}$ $\mathcal{E}$

$\mathcal{E}$ $\mathcal{E}$ $\mathcal{E}$ $\mathcal{E}$ $\mathcal{E}$ $\mathcal{E}$ $\mathcal{E}$ $\mathcal{E}$ $\mathcal{E}$ $\mathcal{E}$

$\mathcal{E}$ $\mathcal{E}$ $\mathcal{E}$ $\mathcal{E}$ $\mathcal{E}$ $\mathcal{E}$ $\mathcal{E}$ $\mathcal{E}$ $\mathcal{E}$

$\mathcal{R}$

ℓ ℓ ℓ ℓ ℓ ℓ

ℓ ℓ ℓ ℓ ℓ ℓ

ℓ ℓ ℓ ℓ ℓ ℓ ℓ ℓ

ℓ ℓ ℓ ℓ ℓ ℓ ℓ ℓ

12

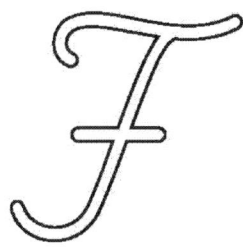

F F F F F

F F F F F

F F F F F F F F F

F F F F F F F F F

F F F F F F F F F

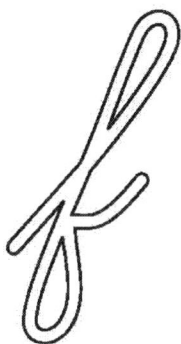

f f f f f f

f f f f f f

f f f f f f f f f

f f f f f f f f f

f f f f f f f f f

6

H

H H H H H H

H H H H H H

H H H H H H H

H H H H H H H

H H H H H H H

h

h h h h h h

h h h h h h

h h h h h h h

h h h h h h h

h h h h h h h

l

l *l* *l* *l* *l* *l*

l *l* *l* *l* *l* *l*

l *l* *l* *l* *l* *l* *l* *l* *l*

l *l* *l* *l* *l* *l* *l* *l* *l*

l *l* *l* *l* *l* *l* *l* *l* *l*

i

i *i* *i* *i* *i* *i*

i *i* *i* *i* *i* *i*

i *i* *i* *i* *i* *i* *i* *i* *i*

i *i* *i* *i* *i* *i* *i* *i* *i*

i *i* *i* *i* *i* *i* *i* *i* *i*

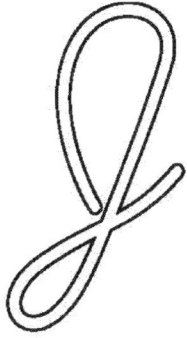
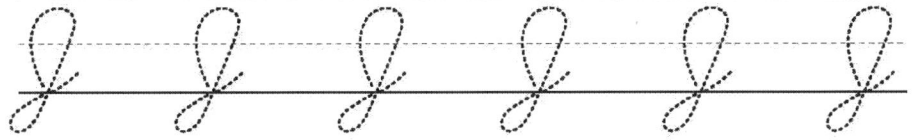
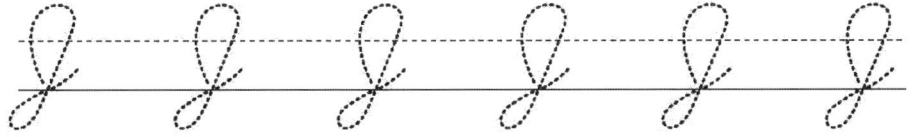
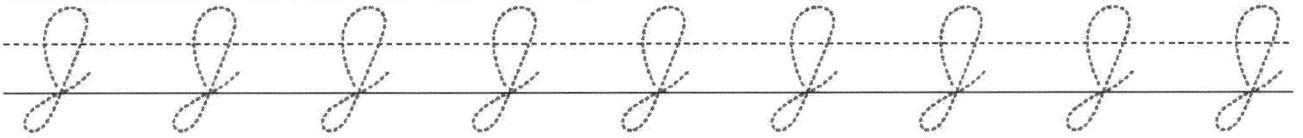
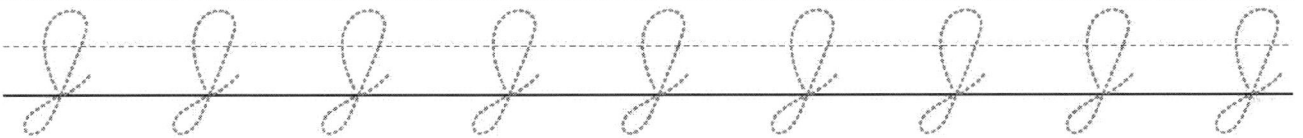
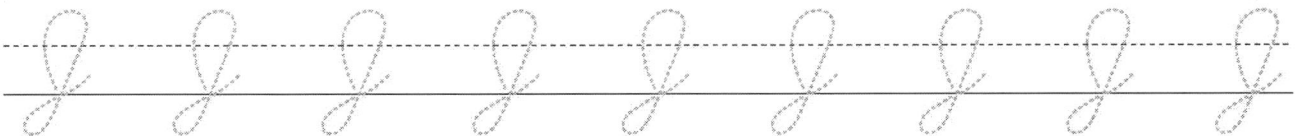

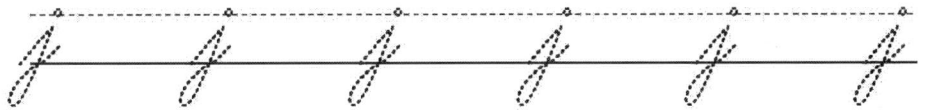
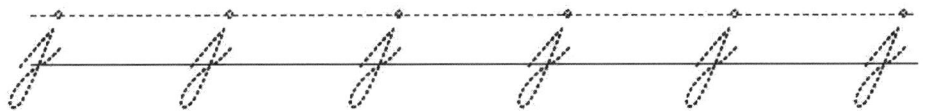
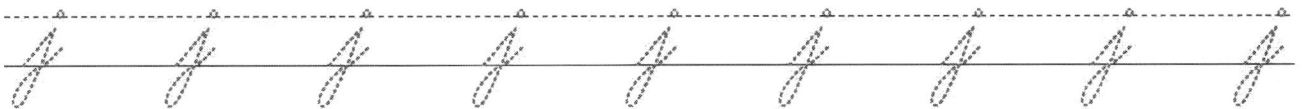
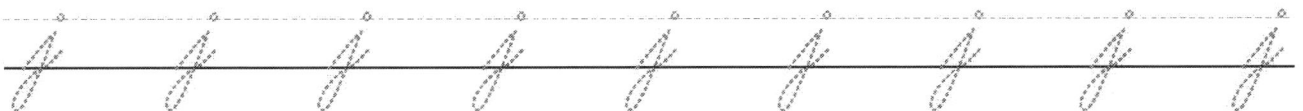
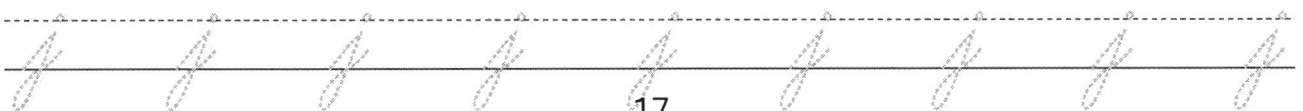

$\mathcal{K}$

$\mathcal{K}\ \mathcal{K}\ \mathcal{K}\ \mathcal{K}\ \mathcal{K}\ \mathcal{K}$

$\mathcal{K}\ \mathcal{K}\ \mathcal{K}\ \mathcal{K}\ \mathcal{K}\ \mathcal{K}$

$\mathcal{K}\ \mathcal{K}\ \mathcal{K}\ \mathcal{K}\ \mathcal{K}\ \mathcal{K}\ \mathcal{K}\ \mathcal{K}\ \mathcal{K}$

$\mathcal{K}\ \mathcal{K}\ \mathcal{K}\ \mathcal{K}\ \mathcal{K}\ \mathcal{K}\ \mathcal{K}\ \mathcal{K}$

$\mathcal{K}\ \mathcal{K}\ \mathcal{K}\ \mathcal{K}\ \mathcal{K}\ \mathcal{K}\ \mathcal{K}\ \mathcal{K}$

k

$k\ k\ k\ k\ k\ k$

$k\ k\ k\ k\ k\ k$

$k\ k\ k\ k\ k\ k\ k\ k\ k$

$k\ k\ k\ k\ k\ k\ k\ k\ k$

$k\ k\ k\ k\ k\ k\ k\ k\ k$

$\mathcal{L}$

$\mathscr{L}$ $\mathscr{L}$ $\mathscr{L}$ $\mathscr{L}$ $\mathscr{L}$ $\mathscr{L}$

$\mathscr{L}$ $\mathscr{L}$ $\mathscr{L}$ $\mathscr{L}$ $\mathscr{L}$ $\mathscr{L}$

$\mathscr{L}$ $\mathscr{L}$ $\mathscr{L}$ $\mathscr{L}$ $\mathscr{L}$ $\mathscr{L}$ $\mathscr{L}$ $\mathscr{L}$ $\mathscr{L}$

$\mathscr{L}$ $\mathscr{L}$ $\mathscr{L}$ $\mathscr{L}$ $\mathscr{L}$ $\mathscr{L}$ $\mathscr{L}$ $\mathscr{L}$ $\mathscr{L}$

$\mathscr{L}$ $\mathscr{L}$ $\mathscr{L}$ $\mathscr{L}$ $\mathscr{L}$ $\mathscr{L}$ $\mathscr{L}$ $\mathscr{L}$ $\mathscr{L}$

$\mathcal{l}$

l l l l l l

l l l l l l

l l l l l l l l l

l l l l l l l l l

l l l l l l l l l

ℳ

ℳ ℳ ℳ ℳ ℳ ℳ ℳ

ℳ ℳ ℳ ℳ ℳ ℳ ℳ

ℳ ℳ ℳ ℳ ℳ ℳ ℳ ℳ ℳ

ℳ ℳ ℳ ℳ ℳ ℳ ℳ ℳ

ℳ ℳ ℳ ℳ ℳ ℳ ℳ ℳ

m

m m m m m m

m m m m m m

m m m m m m m m m

m m m m m m m m m

m m m m m m m m m

n

𝓃 𝓃 𝓃 𝓃 𝓃 𝓃

𝓃 𝓃 𝓃 𝓃 𝓃 𝓃

𝓃 𝓃 𝓃 𝓃 𝓃 𝓃 𝓃 𝓃

𝓃 𝓃 𝓃 𝓃 𝓃 𝓃 𝓃 𝓃

𝓃 𝓃 𝓃 𝓃 𝓃 𝓃 𝓃 𝓃

m

𝓂 𝓂 𝓂 𝓂 𝓂 𝓂

𝓂 𝓂 𝓂 𝓂 𝓂 𝓂

𝓂 𝓂 𝓂 𝓂 𝓂 𝓂 𝓂 𝓂

𝓂 𝓂 𝓂 𝓂 𝓂 𝓂 𝓂 𝓂

O O O O O O

O O O O O O

O O O O O O O O O

O O O O O O O O O

O O O O O O O O O

o o o o o o

o o o o o o

o o o o o o o o o

o o o o o o o o o

P

p p p p p p
p p p p p p
p p p p p p p p
p p p p p p p p
p p p p p p p p

p

p p p p p p
p p p p p p

p p p p p p p p

p p p p p p p p

p p p p p p p p

23

24

R

R R R R R R
R R R R R R
R R R R R R R R
R R R R R R R R
R R R R R R R R

n

n n n n n n
n n n n n n
n n n n n n n n
n n n n n n n n
n n n n n n n n

25

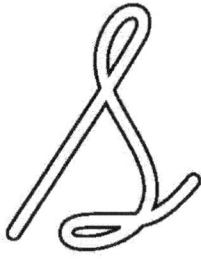

テ

た

𝒰

𝒰 𝒰 𝒰 𝒰 𝒰 𝒰
𝒰 𝒰 𝒰 𝒰 𝒰 𝒰

𝒰 𝒰 𝒰 𝒰 𝒰 𝒰 𝒰
𝒰 𝒰 𝒰 𝒰 𝒰 𝒰 𝒰
𝒰 𝒰 𝒰 𝒰 𝒰 𝒰 𝒰

𝓊

Uu Uu Uu Uu Uu Uu
Uu Uu Uu Uu Uu Uu

Uu Uu Uu Uu Uu Uu Uu Uu Uu
Uu Uu Uu Uu Uu Uu Uu Uu Uu
Uu Uu Uu Uu Uu Uu Uu Uu Uu

$\mathcal{V}$ $\mathcal{V}$ $\mathcal{V}$ $\mathcal{V}$ $\mathcal{V}$ $\mathcal{V}$ $\mathcal{V}$ $\mathcal{V}$

$\mathcal{X}$

$\mathcal{X}$ $\mathcal{X}$ $\mathcal{X}$ $\mathcal{X}$ $\mathcal{X}$ $\mathcal{X}$

$\mathcal{X}$ $\mathcal{X}$ $\mathcal{X}$ $\mathcal{X}$ $\mathcal{X}$ $\mathcal{X}$

$\mathcal{X}$ $\mathcal{X}$ $\mathcal{X}$ $\mathcal{X}$ $\mathcal{X}$ $\mathcal{X}$ $\mathcal{X}$ $\mathcal{X}$ $\mathcal{X}$

$\mathcal{X}$ $\mathcal{X}$ $\mathcal{X}$ $\mathcal{X}$ $\mathcal{X}$ $\mathcal{X}$ $\mathcal{X}$ $\mathcal{X}$

$\mathcal{X}$ $\mathcal{X}$ $\mathcal{X}$ $\mathcal{X}$ $\mathcal{X}$ $\mathcal{X}$ $\mathcal{X}$ $\mathcal{X}$ $\mathcal{X}$

x

x x x x x x

x x x x x x

x x x x x x x x x

x x x x x x x x x

x x x x x x x x x

Y

Y y y y y y y
Y y y y y y y
y y y y y y y y y
y y y y y y y y y
y y y y y y y y y

y

y y y y y y
y y y y y y
y y y y y y y y y
y y y y y y y y y
y y y y y y y y y

33

Practice writing these letters one at a time.

A B C D E F G H I

J K L M N O P Q

R S T U V W X Y Z

Practice writing these letters one at a time.

a b c d e f g h i

j k l m n o p q r

s t u v w x y z

Practice writing these letters one at a time.

$\mathcal{A}\ \mathcal{B}\ \mathcal{C}\ \mathcal{D}\ \mathcal{E}\ \mathcal{F}\ \mathcal{G}\ \mathcal{H}\ \mathcal{I}$

$\mathcal{J}\ \mathcal{K}\ \mathcal{L}\ \mathcal{M}\ \mathcal{N}\ \mathcal{O}\ \mathcal{P}\ \mathcal{Q}$

$\mathcal{R}\ \mathcal{S}\ \mathcal{T}\ \mathcal{U}\ \mathcal{V}\ \mathcal{W}\ \mathcal{X}\ \mathcal{Y}\ \mathcal{Z}$

Practice writing these letters one at a time.

a b c d e f g h i

j k l m n o p q r

s t u v w x y z

Practice writing these letters one at a time.

$\mathcal{A}$ $\mathcal{B}$ $\mathcal{C}$ $\mathcal{D}$ $\mathcal{E}$ $\mathcal{F}$ $\mathcal{G}$ $\mathcal{H}$ $\mathcal{I}$

$\mathcal{J}$ $\mathcal{K}$ $\mathcal{L}$ $\mathcal{M}$ $\mathcal{N}$ $\mathcal{O}$ $\mathcal{P}$ $\mathcal{Q}$

$\mathcal{R}$ $\mathcal{S}$ $\mathcal{T}$ $\mathcal{U}$ $\mathcal{V}$ $\mathcal{W}$ $\mathcal{X}$ $\mathcal{Y}$ $\mathcal{Z}$

Practice writing these letters one at a time.

a b c d e f g h i

j k l m n o p q r

s t u v w x y z

Practice writing these letters one at a time.

$\mathcal{A}$ $\mathcal{B}$ $\mathcal{C}$ $\mathcal{D}$ $\mathcal{E}$ $\mathcal{F}$ $\mathcal{G}$ $\mathcal{H}$ $\mathcal{I}$

$\mathcal{J}$ $\mathcal{K}$ $\mathcal{L}$ $\mathcal{M}$ $\mathcal{N}$ $\mathcal{O}$ $\mathcal{P}$ $\mathcal{Q}$

$\mathcal{R}$ $\mathcal{S}$ $\mathcal{T}$ $\mathcal{U}$ $\mathcal{V}$ $\mathcal{W}$ $\mathcal{X}$ $\mathcal{Y}$ $\mathcal{Z}$

Practice writing these letters one at a time.

a b c d e f g h i

j k l m n o p q r

s t u v w x y z

PART 2

Word Practice

Practice tracing and writing the various 1-2 word phrases. Be mindful of your pen stroke and rhythm as you trace the letters.

Them Them

that that

Your Your

Only Only

for for

the the

They They

was was

Have   *have*

this   *this*

That   *That*

Can't   *Can't*

what   *what*

Who   *Who*

would   *would*

gets   *gets*

There *there*

which *which*

people *people*

take *take*

could *could*

Into *Into*

Just *Just*

which *which*

Their *Their*

also me *also me*

here *here*

think *think*

look *look*

those *those*

Even *Even*

good *good*

Other *Other*

more *more*

These *These*

More *More*

Want *Want*

Like *Like*

way in *way in*

look *look*

48

I can I can

Please Please

house house

Little Little

Soon Soon

Sister Sister

Mother Mother

Dad Dad

I'm here I'm here

Go now Go now

Mine Mine

I see I see

for for

Bye bye

hurry hurry

I do I do

Kiss me Kiss me

Oh no! Oh no!

What? What?

Lets go Lets go

hug me hug me

LOL LOL

moved moved

Lovely Lovely

Love   Love

I won't   I won't

Cool   Cool

Only   Only

sweet   sweet

pretty   pretty

Sweet   Sweet

OMG   OMG

PART 3

Practice Writing Through Famous, Inspirational Quotes

Get uplifted as you relax with motivational quotes to live by

Every moment is a
fresh beginning.
T.S. Eliot

Never regret anything
that made you smile.
Mark Twain

Whatever you do,
do it well.
Walt Disney

What we think,
we become.
Buddha

Reality is wrong,
dreams are for real.
Tupac

Never let your
emotions overpower
your intelligence.
Drake

It hurt because
it mattered.
John Green

When words fail
music speaks.
Shakespeare

Tough times never last
but tough people do.
Robert H. Schuller

Yesterday you
said tomorrow.

Just do it.
Nike

PART 4

Practice with
Famous Song Lyrics

Trace and copy beautiful, motivational
song lyrics through the ages.

Hello darkness, my old friend, I've come to talk with you again - Simon and Garfunkel "The Sounds of Silence"

2

But time makes you bolder,
even children get older
and I'm gettin' older
too. - Fleetwood Mac
"Landslide"

"And, if you listen very hard, the tune will come to you at last. When all are one and one is all, to be a rock and not to roll. And she's buying a stairway to Heaven."

Led Zeppelin, "Stairway to Heaven"

"I see friends shaking hands,
saying, 'How do you do,'
They're really saying, 'I love
you.'"
— Louis Armstrong, "What a
Wonderful World"

"Many times I've been alone, and many times I've cried. Anyway, you'll never know the many ways I've tried. And still they lead me back to the long, winding road."

— The Beatles, "The Long and Winding Road"

"I've been cheated by you since I don't know when, so I made up my mind, it must come to an end
— Abba, Mamma Mia

On a dark desert highway, cool
wind in my hair, warm
smell of colitas rising up
through the air.
— The Eagles, Hotel California

I fell into a burning ring of fire. i went down down down and the flames went higher

— Johnny Cash, Ring of Fire

"He says, 'Son, can you play me a memory? I'm not really sure how it goes. But it's sad and it's sweet and I knew it complete when I wore a younger man's clothes.'"
— Billy Joel, "Piano Man"

"You can't always get what you want. But, if you try sometimes, you find you get what you need." — The Rolling Stones, "You Can't Always Get What You Want"

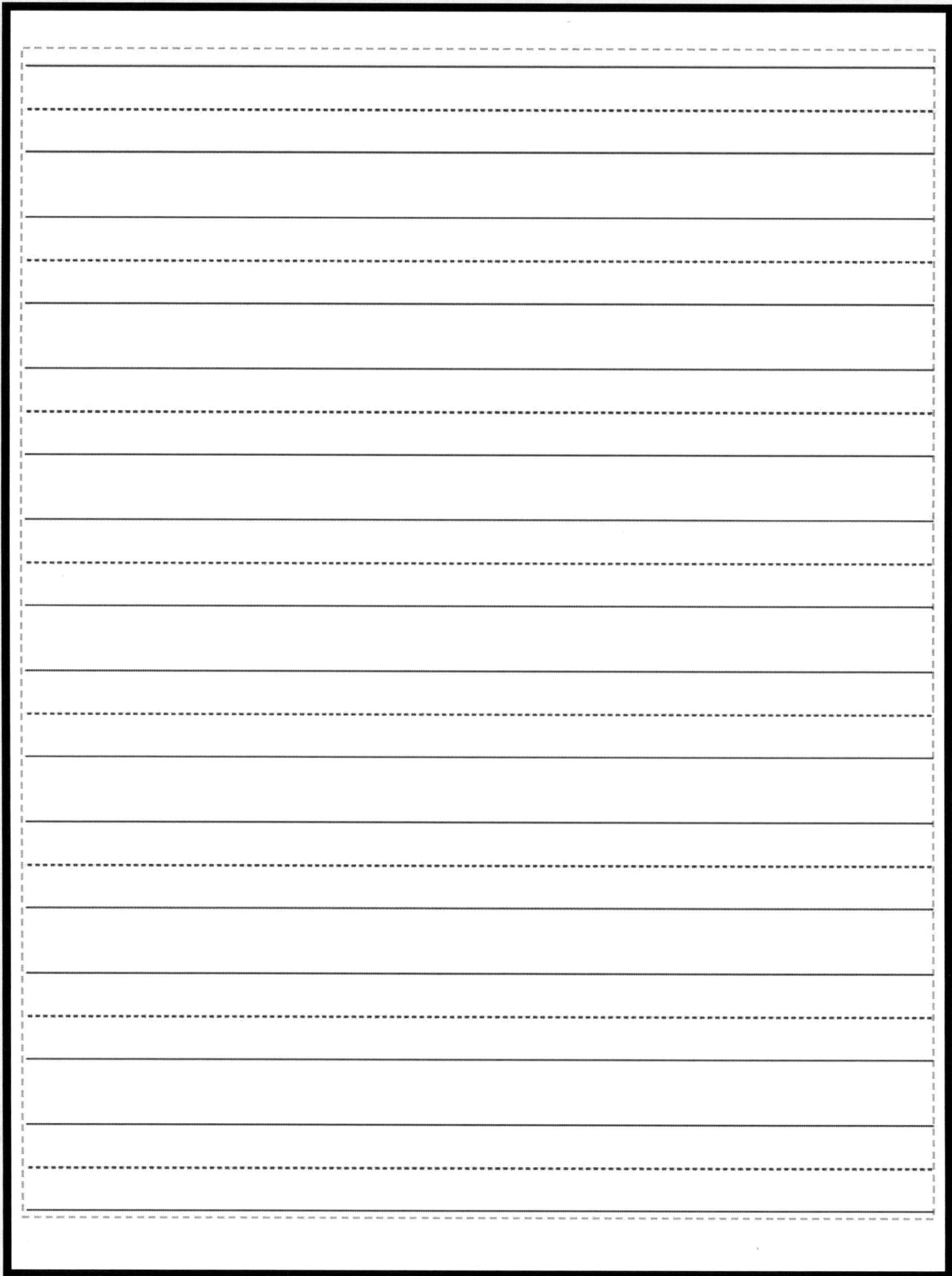

PART 5

Modern Cursive Practice

Let's discover your style through various cursive handwriting techniques.

Modern Cursive

Inspirational Quotes

Trace

"I wish all teenagers could filter through songs instead of turning to drugs and alcohol." - Taylor Swift

Practice

Modern Cursive

Inspirational Quotes

Trace

"Never bend your head. Always hold it high. Look the world straight in the eye." - Hellen Keller

Practice

Modern Cursive

Inspirational Quotes

Trace

"We should all celebrate our individuality and not be embarrassed or ashamed of it." – Johnny Depp

Practice

Modern Cursive

Inspirational Quotes

Trace

"Don't be afraid of failure. This is the way to succeed." - LeBron James

Practice

Modern Cursive

Inspirational Quotes

Trace

"Every accomplishment starts with the decision to try" .- unknown

Practice

Modern Cursive

Inspirational Quotes

Trace

"The future belongs to those who believe in the beauty of their dreams."
Eleanor Roosevelt

Practice

Modern Cursive

Inspirational Quotes

Trace

"Note to self: self-love isn't selfish."
-Dua Lipa

Practice

Modern Cursive
Inspirational Quotes

Trace

"If you don't believe in yourself, why is anyone else going to believe in you." – Tom Brady

Practice

Modern Cursive

Inspirational Quotes

Trace

"Never dull your shine for somebody else." – Tyra Banks.

Practice

Modern Cursive

Inspirational Quotes

Trace

"After a while, you learn to ignore the names people call you and just trust who you are." – Shrek

Practice

_ _

_ _

_ _

_ _

Modern Cursive
Inspirational Quotes

Trace

"No matter what you're going through, there's a light at the end of the tunnel." - Demi Lovato

Practice

Modern Cursive
Inspirational Quotes

Trace

"Oh yes, the past can hurt. But you can either run from it or learn from it." — Rafiki, The Lion King.

Practice

Modern Cursive

Inspirational Quotes

Trace

"Always be a first-rate version of yourself, instead of a second-rate version of someone else." – Judy Garland

Practice

PART 6

Motivational Prompts

Use this moment of relaxation to reflect on positive affirmations while you practice your penmanship.

In cursive, list three reasons why you are amazing. How do you show these each day?

Think about your perfect day. What would you do (or not do)? Who would you see (or not see)?

_____

- -

_____

- -

_____

- -

_____

- -

_____

- -

_____

In cursive, how do you feel most like yourself? Are you with certain people or doing certain things?

In cursive, reflect on your proudest moments or accomplishments in the past year. Why were they significant to you?

In cursive, list 10 of your best qualities.

In cursive, list three things you are deeply grateful for today. For each item, describe why it's important to you.

In cursive, what is one thing you can add to your daily routine that will make you feel good? What is stopping you from adding it?

In cursive, think of someone you admire deeply. What specific qualities or actions of theirs inspire you? How can you emulate these qualities in your own life?

In cursive, think about a time when you faced a significant challenge or obstacle in your life. How did you overcome it?

In cursive, think of a limiting belief you've held about yourself or your capabilities. What's one positive affirmation that counters this belief?

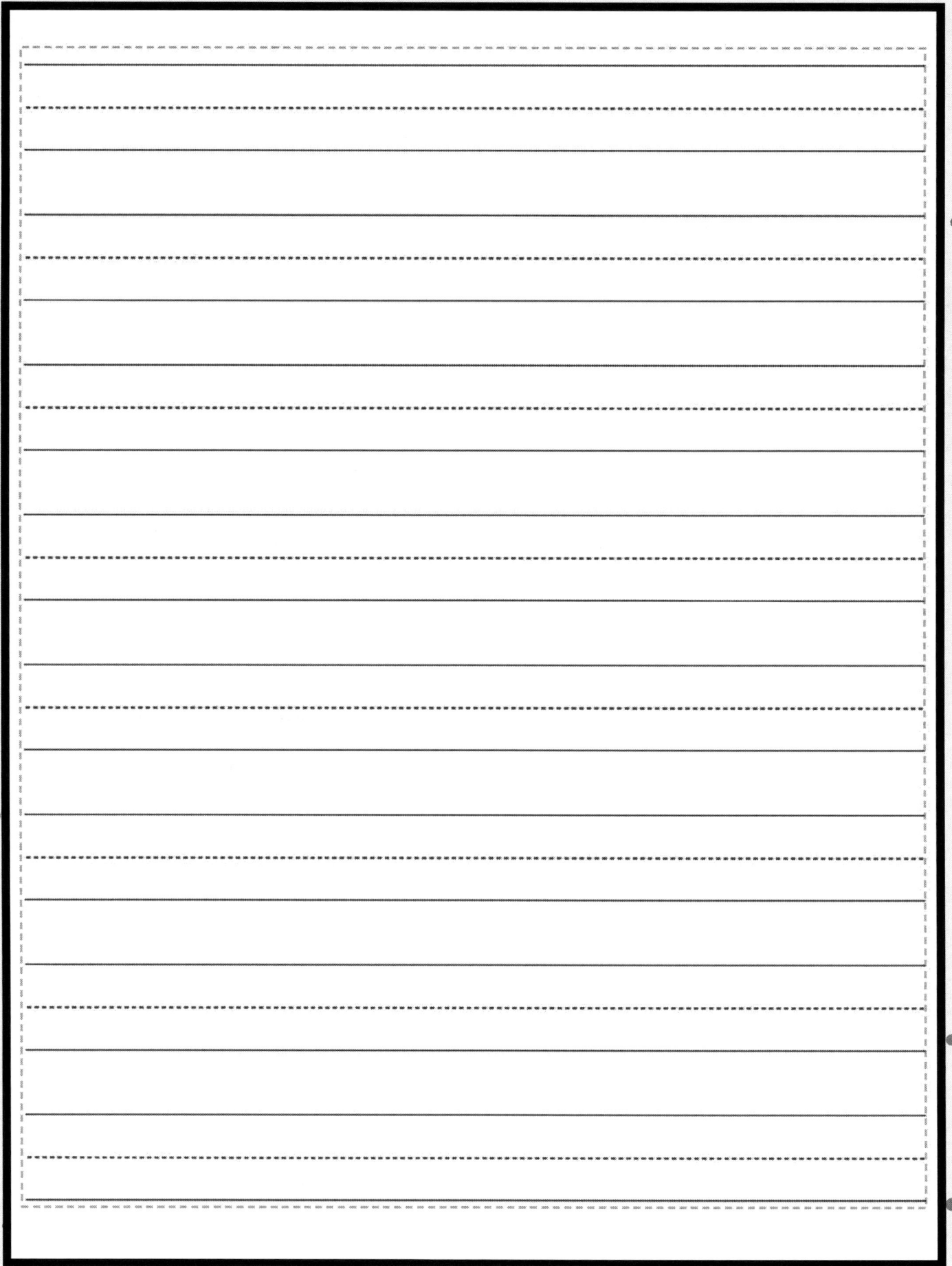

PART 6

Practice Pages

Use these pages to keep practicing and refining your penmanship.

Remember! Practice makes perfect!

100

Creative Works Books

Thank You

We hope you enjoyed this Relaxing Modern Cursive Writing Workbook.

We would be so thankful for a review on Amazon if you have a moment. Doing so will enable us to continue producing new creative books.

Feel free to contact us directly at the link below and let us know how we can improve our products or if you have new ideas for us to develop.

We publish many self-help workbooks, coloring books, anatomy workbooks, handwriting workbooks, and activity books for adults, seniors, teens, and children.

We encourage you to try them all!

Thank you again for your support, and Happy Writing!

www.creativeworksbooks.com

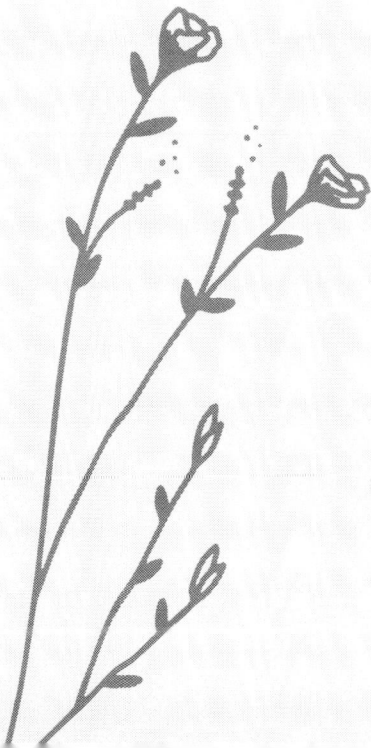

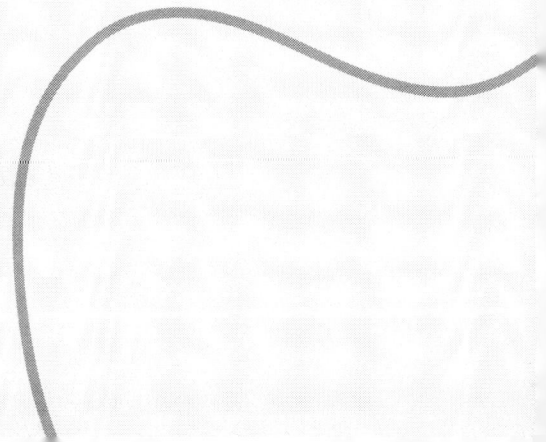